Quick-Crochet

HATS

COMPLETE INSTRUCTIONS FOR 8 STYLES

Creative Publishing
international

contents

Abbreviations

approx	approximately		**patt**	pattern
beg	begin/beginning		**pc**	popcorn
bet	between		**pm**	place marker
BL	back loop(s)		**prev**	previous
BP	back post		**rem**	remain/remaining
BPdc	back post double crochet		**rep**	repeat(s)
CC	contrasting color		**rev sc**	reverse single crochet
ch	chain		**rnd(s)**	round(s)
ch-	refers to chain or space previously made, e.g., ch-1 space		**RS**	right side(s)
ch lp	chain loop		**sc**	single crochet
ch-sp	chain space		**sc2tog**	single crochet 2 stitches together
CL	cluster		**sk**	skip
cm	centimeter(s)		**Sl st**	slip stitch
cont	continue		**sp(s)**	space(s)
dc	double crochet		**st(s)**	stitch(es)
dc2tog	double crochet 2 stitches together		**tbl**	through back loop
dec	decrease/decreases/decreasing		**tch**	turning chain
FL	front loop(s)		**tfl**	through front loop
foll	follow/follows/following		**tog**	together
FP	front post		**tr**	triple crochet
FPdc	front post double crochet		**WS**	wrong side(s)
g	gram(s)		**yd**	yard(s)
hdc	half double crochet		**yo**	yarn over
inc	increase/increases/increasing		**yoh**	yarn over hook
lp(s)	loop(s)		**[ ]**	Work instructions within brackets as many times as directed
m	meter(s)		**( )**	At end of row, indicates total number of stitches worked
MC	main color		*****	Repeat instructions following the single asterisk as directed
mm	millimeter(s)		******	Repeat instructions between asterisks as many times as directed or repeat from a given set of instructions
oz	ounce(s)			
p	picot			

Silky Cloche

This is a classic cloche to wear spring through fall. You can wear the brim down or flipped up on the front, side, or all around. Add flair with a bright flower if you like.

YARN
Lightweight silk/wool blend yarn for hat
330 yd (303 m)
Medium weight ribbon yarn for flower

HOOKS
9/I (5.5 mm)
8/H (5 mm)

STITCH USED
Single crochet

GAUGE
3½ sc = 1" (2.5 cm)
on 9/I hook

NOTIONS
Stitch marker
Tapestry needle

FINISHED SIZE
20" to 22" (51 to 56 cm)
head circumference

Lightweight silk/wool blend yarn in single crochet.

HAT

Hat is worked with double strand throughout.

Foundation rnd: Using 9/I hook, ch 4, join with Sl st to form ring.

Rnd 1: Work 8 sc in ring, pm for beg of rnds, carry marker up at end of each rnd.

Rnd 2: Work 2 sc in each st around (16 sc).

Rnd 3: * Work 1 sc in next st, 2 sc in next st, rep from * around (24 sc).

Rnd 4: * Work 1 sc in each of next 2 sts, 2 sc in next st, rep from * around (32 sc).

Rnd 5: * Work 1 sc in each of next 3 sts, 2 sc in next st, rep from * around (40 sc).

Rnd 6: * Work 1 sc in each of next 4 sts, 2 sc in next st, rep from * around (48 sc).

Rnd 7: * Work 1 sc in each of next 5 sts, 2 sc in next st, rep from * around (56 sc).

Rnd 8: * Work 1 sc in each of next 6 sts, 2 sc in next st, rep from * around (64 sc).

Rnds 9–18: Work even.

Rnd 19 (first inc rnd): * Work 1 sc in each of next 3 sts, 2 sc in next st, rep from * around, end 2 sc in last st (80 sc).

Rnds 20–28: Work even.

Rnds 29–32: Change to 8/H hook. Work even.

Rnd 33 (second inc rnd): Change back to 9/I hook. * Work 1 sc in each of next 9 sts, 2 sc in next st, rep from * around (90 sc).

Rnds 34–41: Work even, end last rnd with Sl st, fasten off, weave in ends using tapestry needle.

ROSE

Foundation rnd: Using 5/F hook, ch 4, join with Sl st to form ring.

Rnd 1: Work 12 sc in ring, join with Sl st to first sc, ch 1.

Rnd 2: Sc in same sc, * ch 3, sk 1, sc in next sc, rep from * around, end ch 3, sk 1 sc, and join in first st (7 lps).

Rnd 3: * In next ch lp, work [sc, hdc, 3 dc, hdc, sc], rep from * around, end Sl st in first sc, fasten off.

Rnd 4: Working in back of petals (in the skipped sc), join yarn in BL of sc on the second rnd below last and first petals, * ch 5, sc tbl of next sc on second rnd below next 2 petals, rep from * around, end ch 5, sc in joining st.

Rnd 5: In next ch lp, work [sc, hdc, 5 dc, hdc, sc], rep from * around, end Sl st in first sc, fasten off, weave in ends using tapestry needle. Attach rose to hat.

Peach Cooler

This is a fresh style for spring and summer. The brim can be folded up or rolled. It will hold its shape because it is crocheted with two strands of cotton.

YARN
Lightweight cotton yarn in two colors

Color A: 216 yd (200 m)
Color B: 216 yd (200 m)

HOOKS
9/I (5.5 mm)
6/G (4 mm)

STITCH USED
Single crochet

GAUGE
14 sc = 4" (10 cm) on
9/I hook

NOTIONS
Stitch marker
Tapestry needle

FINISHED SIZE
20" to 21" (51 to 53.5 cm)
head circumference

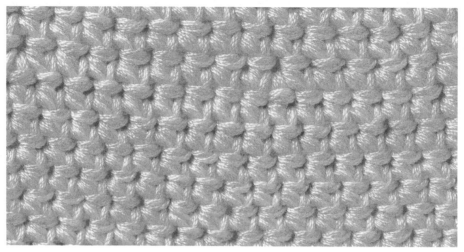

Two strands of lightweight cotton yarn in slightly different shades worked together in single crochet.

HAT

Hat is worked with one strand of each yarn held tog throughout. WS of sc is used as RS of hat.

Foundation rnd: Using 9/I hook, ch 4, join with Sl st to form ring. Work 8 sc in ring, pm after eighth st, do not join, do not ch, carry marker up at end of each rnd.

Rnd 1: * Work 2 sc in next st, rep from * around (16 sc).

Rnd 2: * Work 1 sc in next st, 2 sc in next st, rep from * around (24 sc).

Rnd 3: * Work 1 sc in each of next 2 sts, 2 sc in next st, rep from * around (32 sc).

Rnd 4: * Work 1 sc in each of next 3 sts, 2 sc in next st, rep from * around (40 sc).

Rnd 5: * Work 1 sc in each of next 4 sts, 2 sc in next st, rep from * around (48 sc).

Rnds 6 and 7: * Work 1 sc in next st, rep from * around (48 sc).

Rnd 8: * Work 1 sc in each of next 5 sts, 2 sc in next st, rep from * around (56 sc).

Rnds 9 and 10: Rep rnds 6 and 7.

Rows of tight single crochet stitches cause the hat brim to roll.

Rnd 11: * Work 1 sc in each of next 6 sts, 2 sc in next st, rep from * around (64 sc).

Rnds 12 and 13: Rep rnds 6 and 7.

Rnd 14: * Work 1 sc in each of next 7 sts, 2 sc in next st, rep from * around (72 sc).

Rnds 15–28: Rep rnd 6, join with Sl st, and turn, reversing direction.

Start rolled brim as follows:

Rnd 29 (first inc row): * Work 1 sc in each of next 17 sts, 2 sc in next st, rep from * around (76 sc).

Rnd 30: Rep rnd 6.

Rnd 31 (second inc row): Work 1 sc in each of next 2 sts, * 1 sc in each of next 7 sts, 2 sc in next st, rep from * around, end sc in each of last 2 sts (85 sc).

Rnd 32: Rep rnd 6.

Rnd 33 (third inc row): Work 1 sc in next st, * 1 sc in each of next 6 sts, 2 sc in next st, rep from * around (99 sc).

Rnd 34: Change to 6/G hook. Rep rnd 6 (this tightens brim, causing it to roll up), fasten off, weave in ends using tapestry needle.

New Plaid Tam

Everyone is mad about plaid, and a jaunty tam is the ultimate plaid accessory. Did you know you could make plaid with crochet? The raised bars on this hat are made with front post double crochet. Don't be intimidated; you'll pick up the pattern quickly once you start.

YARN
Medium-weight acrylic yarn
315 yd (290 m)
Bulky-weight ribbon yarn
100 yd (92 m)

HOOKS
6/G (4 mm)
9/I (5.5 mm)
10/J (6 mm)

STITCHES USED
Single crochet
Half double crochet
Front post double crochet
Reverse single crochet

GAUGE
16 sc = 4" (10 cm) on
6/G hook
14 hdc = 4" (10 cm) on
9/I hook
11 hdc = 4" (10 cm) on
10/J hook

NOTIONS
Stitch marker
Tapestry needle
8" (20.5 cm) piece of cardboard

FINISHED SIZE
20" (51 cm)
head circumference

Ribbon yarn in single crochet forms raised bars in the plaid design.

HAT

Foundation rnd: Using 6/G hook and MC, starting with band, ch 76. Being careful not to twist, join with Sl st to form ring. Using a CC yarn, pm.

Rnd 1: Sc in each ch around, carry up marker now and at end of every rnd of band.

Rnd 2: Sc in each st around.

Rnds 3, 4, and 5: Rep rnd 2.

Rnd 6: Work 1 sc in first st, 2 sc in next st (inc made), * sc in each of next 8 sts, inc in next st, rep from * 7 times more, sc in each of last 2 sts (85 sc). End of band.

Change to 9/I hook and begin crown as follows:

Rnd 1: Ch 2 (counts as first hdc now and throughout), work 1 hdc in each st around (85 hdc), join with Sl st to top of beg ch 2.

Rnd 2: Ch 2, work 1 hdc in each of next 5 sts, * 1 FPdc over next hdc, 1 hdc in next st, 1 FPdc over next hdc, 1 hdc in each of next 11 sts, rep from * 4 times more, 1 FPdc over next hdc, 1 hdc in next st, 1 FPdc over next hdc, 1 hdc in each of next 6 sts, join with Sl st to top of beg ch 2, join CC, ch 2 (at end of this rnd, there will be 6 hdc at beg, 6 raised ribs with 11 hdc bet, 6 hdc at end).

Rnd 3: With CC, rep rnd 2, ch 2 with MC.

Rnds 4–7: Change to 10/J hook. With MC, rep rnd 2. At end of rnd 7, ch 2 with CC.

Rnd 8: With CC, rep rnd 2, ch 2 with MC.

Rnd 9 (first dec row): With MC, ch 2, work 1 hdc in each of next 3 sts, dec over next 2 sts (to dec, hdc, yo pick up lp in next st, yo pick up lp in next st, yo through all 5 lps on hook), * 1 FPdc over next FPdc, 1 hdc next st, 1 FPdc over next FPdc, dec over next 2 sts, 1 hdc in each of next 7 sts, dec over next 2 sts, rep from * 4 times, 1 FPdc, 1 hdc, 1 FPdc, dec over next 2 sts, 1 hdc in each of rem 4 sts, join with Sl st to top of beg ch 2 (73 sts).

Rnd 10: With MC, foll patt as established.

Rnd 11 (second dec row): With MC, dec 1 st before and after each raised rib (61 sts).

Rnd 12: With MC, foll patt as established.

Rnd 13 (3rd dec row): With CC, dec 1 st before and after each raised rib (49 sts).

Rnd 14: With MC, foll patt as established.

Rnd 15 (4th dec row): With MC, dec 1 st before and after each raised rib (37 sts).

Rnd 16: With MC, foll patt as established.

Rnd 17 (5th dec row): With MC, ch 2, work 1 FPdc, 1 hdc, 1 FPdc, * dec over next 2 sts , 1 hdc, 1 FPdc, 1 hdc, 1 FPdc, rep from * ending with Sl st to top of beg ch 2.

Rnd 18: With CC, ch 2, foll patt as established.

Rnd 19: With MC, ch 2, * work 1 FPdc, 1 hdc, 1 FPdc, 1 hdc, rep from * ending with Sl st in top of beg ch 2.

Rnd 20: With MC, ch 2, * work 1 FPdc, sk hdc, rep from * ending with Sl st in top of beg ch 2, fasten off, leaving an 18" (46 cm) end.

FINISHING

1. Using tapestry needle, draw long end through top of last row and pull up tight, knot, fasten off, weave in ends.
2. With CC and 9/I hook, work sc from top to bottom over each row of FPdc, forming vertical rows of plaid, weave in ends.
3. With MC and 6/G hook, work 1 row of sc and 1 row of rev sc around bottom of band, weave in ends.
4. To create tassel, wrap ribbon around an 8" (20.5 cm) piece of cardboard about 15 times. Thread a piece of ribbon under the loops at the top and tie tightly. Slip the loops off the cardboard. Tie another piece of ribbon around the loops 1" (2.5 cm) down from the top. Cut the loops at the other end. Tie the tassel to the cap point.

Big Stripes Beanie

This cap has wide stripes and an interesting texture created by crocheting through the back loop of the stitches. You can never have enough caps!

YARN
Medium-weight acrylic yarn in three colors: 1 skein each

HOOK
9/I (5.5 mm)

STITCHES USED
Single crochet
Double crochet
Double crochet through back loop

GAUGE
12 dc = 4" (10 cm)

NOTION
Tapestry needle

FINISHED SIZE
20" to 22" (51 to 56 cm) head circumference

Medium-weight acrylic yarn in double crochet worked through back loop.

CAP

Foundation rnd: Using A, ch 4, join with Sl st to form ring.

Rnd 1: Ch 3 (counts as dc now and throughout), work 9 dc in ring, join with Sl st to top of beg ch 3.

Rnd 2: Ch 3, working tbl of each st now and throughout, 1 dc in same st as ch 3, 2 dc in each rem st around, join with Sl st to top of beg ch 3 (20 dc).

Rnd 3: Ch 3, work 2 dc in next st, * 1 dc in next st, 2 dc in next st, rep from * around, join with Sl st to top of beg ch 3 (30 dc).

Rnd 4: Ch 3, work 1 dc in next st, 2 dc in next st, * 1 dc in each of next 2 sts, 2 dc in next st, rep from * around, join with Sl st to top of beg ch 3 (40 dc), fasten off A.

Rnd 5: Join B, ch 3, work 1 dc in each of next 2 sts, 2 dc in next st, * 1 dc in each of next 3 sts, 2 dc in next st, rep from * around, join with Sl st to top of beg ch 3 (50 dc).

Rnd 6: Ch 3, work 1 dc in each of next 3 sts, 2 dc in next st, * 1 dc in each of next 4 sts, 2 dc in next st, rep from * around, join with Sl st to top of beg ch 3 (60 dc).

Rnds 7 and 8: Ch 3, work 1 dc in each st around, join with Sl st to top of beg ch 3, fasten off B.

Rnds 9–11: Join C at beg of rnd 9, rep rnd 7, but do not fasten off C.

Rnds 12–18: Ch 1 (counts as sc now and throughout), sk first st, work 1 sc in each st around, join with Sl st to beg ch 1, fasten off C.

FINISHING
Weave in ends using tapestry needle.

The Newsboy

Extra, extra, read all about it! This is an urban look with lots of attitude. The Newsboy has a great ribbed texture. The reverse side of the stitches is actually on the outside (thanks to Johnny, who told me it looked cooler that way). The ribs are formed by front post double crochet stitches, and the double crochet stitches between the ribs are worked in the spaces rather than the stitches. The bill is worked with two strands of yarn for extra stiffness.

YARN
Bulky-weight wool yarn
310 yd (285 m)

HOOK
9/I (5.5 mm)

STITCHES USED
Single crochet
Double crochet
Front post double crochet

GAUGE
10 dc = 4" (10 cm)

NOTION
Tapestry needle

FINISHED SIZE
20" to 21" (51 to 53.5 cm)
head circumference

Ribs formed by front post double crochet stitches; wrong side out.

BILL

Wind off about 12 yd (11 m) of yarn. Hold this yarn together with main skein to crochet bill with a double strand as follows:

Foundation row: Ch 27. Beg in second ch from hook, work 1 sc in each ch to end (26 sc), ch 1, turn.

Rows 1 and 2: Sk first st, * work 1 sc in next st, rep from * across, end 1 sc in tch, ch 1, turn.

Row 3: Sk first st, sc2tog, sc to last 3 sts, sc2tog, sc in last st (24 sc), ch 1, turn.

Row 4: Rep row 3 (22 sc).

Row 5: Rep row 3 (20 sc), fasten off, leaving a long end for sewing. Set cap bill aside.

CAP

Foundation rnd: Ch 4, join with Sl st to form ring, ch 3 (counts as dc now and throughout), work 15 dc in ring (16 dc), join with Sl st to top of ch 3.

Rnd 1: Ch 3, * work 1 FPdc in each of next 2 sts, 1 dc in sp bet last dc worked and next dc (inc made), rep from * 6 times more, 1 FPdc in each of next 2 sts, join with Sl st to top of beg ch 3 (24 dc).

Rnd 2: Ch 3, work 1 dc in next sp, 1 FPdc in each of next 2 FPdc, * 1 dc in next sp, sk dc, 1 dc in next sp, 1 FPdc in each of next 2 FPdc, rep from * 6 times more, join with Sl st to top of beg ch 3 (32 dc).

Rnd 3: Ch 3, work 1 dc in each of next 2 sps, 1 FPdc in each of next 2 FPdc, * 1 dc in each of next 3 sps, 1 FPdc in each of next 2 FPdc, rep from * 6 times more, join with Sl st to top of beg ch 3 (40 dc).

Rnd 4: Ch 3, work 1 dc in each of next 3 sps, 1 FPdc in each of next 2 FPdc, * 1 dc in each of next 4 sps, 1 FPdc in each of next 2 FPdc, rep from * 6 times more, join with Sl st to top of beg ch 3 (48 dc).

Cont to work patt as established, always having 1 more dc bet FPdc ribs, until you have 96 sts.

First dec row: Ch 3, sk 1 sp, dc dec in next 2 sps, 1 dc in each of next 4 sps, 1 dc dec in next 2 sps, 1 dc in next space, 1 FPdc in each of next 2 FPdc, * sk 1 sp, 1 dc next sp, dc dec in next 2 sps, 1 dc in each of next 4 sps, dc dec in next 2 sps, 1 dc in next sp, 1 FPdc in each of next 2 FPdc, rep from * around, join with Sl st to top of beg ch 3 (80 dc).

Second dec row: Ch 3, dc dec in next 2sps, 1 dc in each of next 3 sps, 1 dc dec in next 2 sps, sk 1 sp, 1 FPdc in each of next 2 FPdc, * 1 dc in next sp, 1 dc dec in next 2 sps, 1 dc in each of next 3 sps, 1 dc dec in next 2sps, sk 1 sp, 1 FPdc in each of next 2 FPdc, rep from * around (64 sts).

Third dec row: Ch 1, (working each st instead of sp) sk first st, * work 1 sc in each of next 5 sts, sc2tog , rep from * 8 times more (9 dec in all) (55 sts), join with Sl st to beg ch 1, do not fasten off yarn (this is center back of cap).

FINISHING

1. Pin bill to cap front edge, right sides together, matching centers. Sew pieces together using tapestry needle and long yarn that was left, weave in ends.

2. Pick up yarn at center back, sc along bottom of cap, around edge of bill, and back to where you started. Join with Sl st, fasten off, weave in ends using tapestry needle.

Girl Beanie

The girls like beanies, too, so this one is styled for them.

YARN
Lightweight wool/acrylic
blend yarn in two colors:
1 skein each
162 yd (149 m)

HOOK
9/I (5.5 mm)

STITCHES USED
Single crochet
Double crochet

GAUGE
12 dc = 4" (10 cm)

NOTION
Tapestry needle

FINISHED SIZE
20" to 22" (51 to 56 cm)
head circumference

CAP

Foundation rnd: Using MC, ch 4, join with Sl st to form ring.

Rnd 1: Ch 3 (counts as dc now and throughout), work 9 dc in ring, join with Sl st to top of beg ch 3.

Rnd 2: Ch 3, work 1 dc in same st as ch 3, 2 dc in each rem st around, join with Sl st to top of beg ch 3 (20 dc).

Rnd 3: Ch 3, work 2 dc in next st, * 1 dc in next st, 2 dc in next st, rep from * around, join with Sl st to top of beg ch 3 (30 dc).

Rnd 4: Ch 3, work 1 dc in next st, 2 dc in next st, * 1 dc in each of next 2 sts, 2 dc in next st, rep from * around, join with Sl st to top of beg ch 3 (40 dc).

Rnd 5: Ch 3, work 1 dc in each of next 2 sts, 2 dc in next st, * 1 dc in each of next 3 sts, 2 dc in next st, rep from * around, join with Sl st to top of beg ch 3 (50 dc).

Rnd 6: Ch 3, work 1 dc in each of next 3 sts, 2 dc in next st, * 1 dc in each of next 4 sts, 2 dc in next st, rep from * around, join with Sl st to top of beg ch 3 (60 dc).

Rnds 7–11: Ch 3, work 1 dc in each st around, join with Sl st to top of beg ch 3, do not fasten off MC.

Rnd 12: With CC, ch 1 (counts as sc now and throughout), sk first st, work 1 sc in each st around, join with Sl st to beg ch 1.

Rnd 13: With MC, rep rnd 12.

Rnds 14–18: Rep rnds 12 and 13, fasten off.

FINISHING

Weave in ends using tapestry needle.

YARN
Super bulky weight wool yarn
132 yd (121 m)

HOOK
15/P (10 mm)

STITCH USED
Single crochet

GAUGE
9 sc = 4" (10 cm)

NOTIONS
Stitch marker
Tapestry needle

FINISHED SIZE
20" to 21" (51 to 53.5 cm)
head circumference

Super Bulky Hat

Wear this hat on the coldest days of winter. Hooked from super bulky

wool on a large hook, it's quick and easy to make.

Single crochet rounds without increases shape the brim.

HAT

Foundation rnd: Ch 6, join with Sl st to form ring. Work 6 sc in ring, pm for beg of rnds, carry marker up at end of each rnd.

Rnd 1: Work 2 sc in each st around (12 sc).

Rnd 2: * Work 1 sc in next st, 2 sc in next st (inc made), rep from * around (18 sc).

Rnd 3: * Work 1 sc in each of next 2 sts, 2 sc in next st, rep from * around (24 sc).

Rnd 4: * Work 1 sc in each of next 3 sts, 2 sc in next st, rep from * around (30 sc).

Rnd 5: * Work 1 sc in each of next 4 sts, 2 sc in next st, rep from * around (36 sc).

Rnd 6: * Work 1 sc in each of next 5 sts, 2 sc in next st, rep from * around (42 sc).

Rnd 7: * Work 1 sc in each of next 6 sts, 2 sc in next st, rep from * around (48 sc).

Rnd 8: * Work 1 sc in next st, rep from * around (48 sc). Mark this rnd for start of brim.

Rep rnd 8 until brim is 3" (7.5 cm), fasten off.

FINISHING
Weave in ends using tapestry needle. Roll up brim.

Cotton Candy Scarf Hat

It's a scarf, it's a hat, it's both. This fluffy creation is crocheted in luxurious mohair yarn in an open pattern.

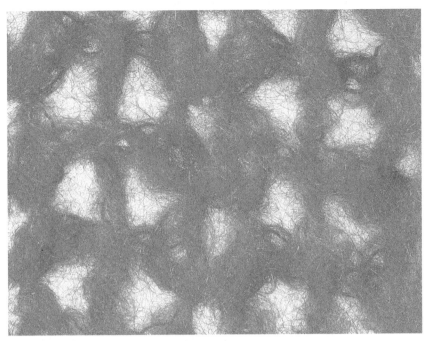

Lacy open-work pattern of double crochet shells and triple crochet stitches.

YARN
Bulky mohair yarn
153 yd (140 m)

HOOK
10½/K (6.5 mm)

STITCHES USED
Double crochet
Triple crochet
Front post triple crochet

GAUGE
2 shells 2 tr = 4" (10 cm)

NOTIONS
Tapestry needle

FINISHED SIZE
10" × 36" (25.5 × 91.5 cm)
head circumference

Make two pieces.

Foundation row: Starting at top, ch 26. Starting in fifth ch from hook, * work 2 dc, ch 2, 2 dc in same ch, sk 2 ch, 1 tr in next ch, sk 2 ch, rep from * until 3 ch rem, sk 2 ch, 1 tr in last ch, ch 4, turn.

Row 1: * Work 2 dc, ch 2, 2 dc in next ch-2 sp, 1 FPtr over bar of tr of prev row, rep from * across, end 1 tr in top of tch, ch 4, turn.

Rep row 1 for 36" (91.5 cm), fasten off.

FINISHING
Using tapestry needle, sew pieces together at top and 10" (25.5 cm) down back. Weave in ends.

CPSIA information can be obtained
at www.ICGtesting.com
Printed in the USA
LVOW06s1008100617

537276LV00007B/4/P